JOSEPH AND THE AMAZING TECHNICOLOR® DREAMCOAT
LYRICS BY TIM RICE • MUSIC BY ANDREW LLOYD WEBBER

All photos are from the New York production starring Michael Damian as Joseph.

Photos: Thompson/Schwartz

Technicolor® is the registered trademark of the Technicolor group of companies.

ISBN 0-7935-3427-5

THE REALLY USEFUL GROUP LTD.

EXCLUSIVELY DISTRIBUTED BY

HAL•LEONARD
CORPORATION
7777 W. BLUEMOUND RD. P.O. BOX 13819 MILWAUKEE, WI 53213

JOSEPH'S DREAMS

37 ³Now Israel loved Joseph more than any of his other sons, because he had been born to him in his old age, and he made a richly ornamented robe for him. ⁴When his brothers saw that their father loved him more than any of them, they hated him and could not speak a kind word to him.

⁵Joseph had a dream and when he told it to his brothers, they hated him all the more.

¹⁸(The brothers) saw him in the distance, and before he reached them, they plotted to kill him.

²³So when Joseph came to his brothers they stripped him of his robe – the richly ornamented robe he was wearing – ²⁴and they took him and threw him into the cistern.

²⁵As they sat down to eat their meal, they looked up and saw a caravan of Ishmaelites coming from Gilead. Their camels were loaded with spices, balm and myrrh, and they were on their way to take them down to Egypt.

²⁸So when the Midianite merchants came by, his brothers pulled Joseph up out of the cistern and sold him for twenty Shekels of silver to the Ishmaelites, who took him to Egypt.

³¹Then they got Joseph's robe, slaughtered a goat and dipped the robe in the blood. ³²They took the ornamented robe back to their father and said, "We found this. Examine it to see whether it is your son's robe."

³³He recognized it and said, "It is my son's robe! Some ferocious animal has devoured him. Joseph has surely been torn to pieces."

JOSEPH AND POTIPHAR'S WIFE

39 ¹Now Joseph had been taken down to Egypt. Potiphar, an Egyptian who was one of the Pharaoh's officials, the captain of the guard, bought him from the Ishmaelites who had taken him there.

⁶Now Joseph was well-built and handsome, ⁷and after a while his master's wife took notice of Joseph and said, "Come to bed with me!"

⁸But he refused.

¹³...she saw that he had left his cloak in her hand and had run out of the house...

²⁰Joseph's master took him and put him in prison...

THE CUPBEARER AND THE BAKER

40 ¹Some time later the cupbearer and the baker of the king of Egypt offended their master, the king of Egypt. ²Pharaoh was angry with his two officials, the chief cupbearer and the chief baker, ³and put them in custody in the house of the captain of the guard, in the same prison where Joseph was confined.

⁵...each of the two men – the cupbearer and the baker of the king of Egypt, who were being held in prison – had a dream the same night, and each dream had a meaning of its own.

⁸"We both had dreams," (they said), "but there is no-one to interpret them."

Then Joseph said to them, "Do not interpretations belong to God? Tell me your dreams."

⁹So the chief cupbearer told Joseph his dream. He said to him, "In my dream I saw a vine in front of me, ¹⁰and on the vine were three branches. As soon as it budded, it blossomed, and its clusters ripened into grapes. ¹¹Pharaoh's cup was in my hand, and I took the grapes, squeezed them into Pharaoh's cup and put the cup in his hand."

¹²"This is what it means," Joseph said to him. "The three branches are three days. ¹³Within three days

Pharaoh will lift up your head and restore you to your position, and you will put Pharaoh's cup in his hand, just as you used to when you were his cupbearer.

¹⁴But when all goes well with you, remember me and show me kindness; mention me to Pharaoh and get me out of this prison."

¹⁶When the chief baker saw that Joseph had given a favourable interpretation, he said to Joseph, "I too had a dream: On my head were three baskets of bread. ¹⁷In the top basket were all kinds of baked goods for Pharaoh, but birds were eating them out of the basket on my head."

¹⁸"This is what it means," Joseph said. "The three baskets are three days. ¹⁹Within three days Pharaoh will lift off your head and hang you on a tree. And the birds will eat away your flesh."

²¹(On the third day Pharaoh) restored the chief cupbearer to his position, so that he once again put the cup into Pharaoh's hand, ²²but he hanged the chief baker, just as Joseph had said to them in his interpretation.

PHARAOH'S DREAMS

41 ¹When two full years had passed, Pharaoh had a dream. He was standing by the Nile, ²when out of the river there came up seven cows, sleek and fat, and they grazed among the reeds. ³After them, seven other cows, ugly and gaunt, came up out of the Nile and stood beside those on the riverbank. ⁴And the cows that were ugly and gaunt ate up the seven sleek, fat cows. Then Pharaoh woke up.

⁵He fell asleep again and had a second dream: Seven ears of corn, healthy and good, were growing on a single stalk. ⁶After them, seven other ears of corn sprouted – thin and scorched by the east wind. ⁷The thin ears of corn swallowed up the seven healthy, full ears. Then Pharaoh woke up; it had been a dream.

⁸In the morning his mind was troubled, so he sent for all the magicians and wise men of Egypt. Pharaoh told them his dreams, but no-one could interpret them for him.

²⁵Then Joseph said to Pharaoh, "The dreams of Pharaoh are one and the same. God has revealed to Pharaoh what he is about to do. ²⁶The seven good cows are seven years, and the seven good ears of corn are seven years: it is one and the same dream. ²⁷The seven lean, ugly cows that came up afterwards are seven years, and so are the seven worthless ears of corn scorched by the east wind: They are seven years of famine.

²⁸"It is just as I said to Pharaoh: God has shown Pharaoh what he is about to do. ²⁹Seven years of great abundance are coming throughout the land of Egypt, ³⁰but seven years of famine will follow them. Then all the abundance in Egypt will be forgotten, and the famine will ravage the land. ³¹The abundance in the land will not be remembered, because the famine that follows it will be so severe."

³⁹The Pharaoh said to Joseph, "Since God has made all this known to you, there is no-one so discerning and wise as you. ⁴⁰You shall be in charge of my palace, and all my people are to submit to your orders. Only with respect to the throne will I be greater than you."

JOSEPH IN CHARGE OF EGYPT

⁴¹So Pharaoh said to Joseph, "I hereby put you in charge of the whole land of Egypt." ⁴²Then Pharaoh took his signet ring and put it on Joseph's finger. He dressed him in robes of fine linen and put a gold chain around his neck. ⁴³He had him ride in a chariot as his second-in-command, and men shouted before him, "Make way!" Thus he put him in charge of the whole land of Egypt.

⁵³The seven years of abundance in Egypt came to an end, ⁵⁴and the seven years of famine began, just as Joseph had said.

⁵⁷And all the countries came to Egypt to buy grain from Joseph, because the famine was severe in the whole world.

JOSEPH'S BROTHERS GO TO EGYPT

42 ⁴So Israel's sons were among those who went to buy grain, for the famine was in the land of Canaan also.

⁷As soon as Joseph saw his brothers, he recognized them, but he pretended to be a stranger and spoke harshly to them.

THE SECOND JOURNEY TO EGYPT

43 ²⁶When Joseph came home, they presented to him the gifts they had brought into the house, and they bowed down before him to the ground. ²⁷He asked them how they were, and then he said, "How is your aged father you told me about? Is he still living?"

²⁸They replied, "Your servant our father is still alive and well." And they bowed low to pay him honour.

²⁹As he looked about and saw his brother Benjamin, his own mother's son, he asked, "Is this your youngest brother, the one you told me about?" And he said "God be gracious to you, my son." ³⁰Deeply moved at the sight of his brother, Joseph hurried out and looked for a place to weep. He went into his private room and wept there. ³¹After he had washed his face, he came out and, controlling himself, said, "Serve the food."

A SILVER CUP IN A SACK

44 ¹Now Joseph gave these instructions to the steward of his house: "Fill the men's sacks with as much food as they can carry, and put each man's silver in the mouth of his sack. ²Then put my cup, the silver one, in the mouth of the youngest one's sack, along with the silver for his grain." And he did as Joseph said.

³As morning dawned, the men were sent on their way with their donkeys. ⁴They had not gone far from the city when Joseph said to his steward, "Go after those men at once, and when you catch up with them, say to them, 'Why have you repaid good with evil? ⁵Isn't this the cup my master drinks from and also uses for divination? This is a wicked thing you have done.'

⁶When he caught up with them he repeated these words to them. ⁷But they said to him, "Why does my lord say such things? Far be it from your servants to do anything like that! ⁸We even brought back to you from the land of Canaan the silver we found inside the mouths of our sacks. So why would we steal silver or gold from your master's house? ⁹If any of your servants is found to have it, he will die; and the rest of us will become my lord's slaves."

¹⁰"Very well, then," he said, "let it be as you say. Whoever is found to have it will become my slave; the rest of you will be free from blame."

¹¹Each of them quickly lowered his sack to the ground and opened it.

¹²Then the steward proceeded to search, beginning with the oldest and ending with the youngest. And the cup was found in Benjamin's sack.

³³[And Judah said] Now then, please let your servant remain here as my lord's slave in place of the boy, and let the boy return with his brothers.

JOSEPH MAKES HIMSELF KNOWN

45 ⁴Then Joseph said to his brothers, "Come close to me." When they had done so, he said, "I am your brother Joseph, the one you sold into Egypt! ⁵And now, do not be distressed and do not be angry with yourselves for selling me here, because it was to save lives that God sent me ahead of you.

¹³"Tell my father about all the honour accorded me in Egypt and about everything you have seen. And bring my father down here quickly."

¹⁵And he kissed all his brothers and wept over them...

JACOB GOES TO EGYPT

46 ²⁹Joseph had his chariot made ready and went to Goshen to meet his father Israel. As soon as Joseph appeared before him, he threw his arms around his father and wept for a long time.

JOSEPH – IT ALL BEGAN IN 1967...

In the summer of 1967, Andrew Lloyd Webber was asked by Alan Doggett, Head of the Music Department at Colet Court, St. Paul's Junior School (who taught his younger brother, Julian) to write a 'pop cantata' for the school choir to sing at their Easter end of term concert.

Andrew immediately approached his friend Tim Rice to ask if he would write lyrics for the project. After toying with ideas about spies, 007s and the like, Tim suggested the story of Joseph.

The first performance of *Joseph and the Amazing Technicolor Dreamcoat* was on a cold winter afternoon on 1st March 1968 at the Old Assembly Hall, Colet Court, Hammersmith. Accompanied by the school orchestra and conducted by Alan Doggett, the performance was only 20 minutes long.

It was such a success that another performance was arranged on 12th May 1968 at Central Hall, Westminster, where Andrew's father was the organist. Julian Lloyd Webber gave a classical recital in the first half, along with Bill Lloyd Webber. The audience of approximately 2,500 consisted mainly of parents of the Colet Court boys. To Andrew and Tim's surprise, Derek Jewell, Jazz and Pop critic for *The Sunday Times*, saw the show and wrote a favourable review of *Joseph*, which appeared on 19th May 1968.

A third performance took place on 9th November 1968 at St. Paul's Cathedral, where *Joseph* was expanded to include songs such as 'Potiphar' for the first time.

After seeing Derek Jewell's review, Tim Rice's then employer Norrie Paramor, who produced Cliff Richard among others, encouraged Decca to release an album of the St. Paul's

Cathedral version of Joseph in January 1969. This received several good reviews, but was unsuccessful commercially.

At the same time as the album's release, Novello & Co. published the original twenty minute version of the music and lyrics.

As a consequence of the obvious need for financial backing to enable them to continue writing, Andrew Lloyd Webber was introduced to Sefton Myers, an entrepreneur keen to develop new talent in showbusiness and whose main activity was property. His partner, David Land, heard the album and immediately offered Tim and Andrew a management contract which would guarantee them support for 3 years in return for a share of their income. This contract allowed Tim and Andrew to continue their work and make it feasible for Tim to leave his employment with Norrie Paramour.

The first project under their new contract was a second piece for schools, entitled *Come Back Richard, Your Country Needs You*, based on the story of Richard I and his minstrel, Blondel. It was performed with Alan Doggett once again as musical director at the City of London School in November 1969, but Andrew and Tim did not take the project further as they had already discussed another idea, the story of Jesus Christ. Tim Rice remained convinced of his second idea for schools and subsequently developed it into the musical *Blondel*.

Andrew Lloyd Webber and Tim Rice then went on to write *Jesus Christ Superstar*. It was the success of *Jesus Christ Superstar* that enabled *Joseph* to continue to grow. The album of *Jesus Christ Superstar* was a

From school hall to West End Stage

massive success in America and when *Joseph* was released there, with a marketing campaign implying it was a follow-up to *Superstar*, the *Joseph* album stayed on the charts for three months.

Sadly, before the success of *Jesus Christ Superstar* had really emerged, Sefton Myers died of cancer. David Land subsequently involved Robert Stigwood in the management contract with Andrew and Tim, which was extended to cover a 10 year period, and a very happy association with David Land on behalf of the Robert Stigwood Organisation followed.

In September 1972 Frank Dunlop for the Young Vic directed the Decca album version of *Joseph* starring Gary Bond, at the Edinburgh Festival, where

it was preceded by an act of medieval mystery plays that led to the story of the 'Coat of Many Colors'. In October the Edinburgh production played at the Young Vic for two weeks before transferring to the Roadhouse for a six week run.

Michael White and Robert Stigwood subsequently presented the Edinburgh *Joseph* at the Albery Theatre, where it opened on 17th February 1973 and was accompanied by a piece called *Jacob's Journey*, written by Tim and Andrew with dialogue by Alan Simpson and Ray Galton. This told the story of the early life of Joseph's father, Jacob. Unfortunately, it was decided that the combination of Jacob's Journey, which contained a lot of spoken dialogue, and *Joseph*, entirely sung, did not work and *Jacob's Journey* was gradually phased out. *Joseph* emerged to receive its first major production in its present form at the Haymarket Theatre, Leicester.

The history of *Joseph* in America is not dissimilar. The first amateur production in America was in May 1970 at the College of the Immaculate Conception in Douglastown, New York. There followed huge interest from colleges and schools but, despite various professional productions including two in New York, it was not until it opened at the Ford Theatre in Washington on 13th April 1980, where it ran for seven months, that *Joseph* had any kind of professional success.

This production was transferred to the Entermedia theatre in New York opening on 13th November 1981 and was so successful that on 27th January 1982 it moved to the Royale Theatre on Broadway.

These many years later, it is intriguing to note that in the year of the first performance the copyright on *Joseph* was sold by Andrew and Tim to Novello & Co. for 50 guineas each. Novello & Co. was subsequently purchased by Filmtrax, who continued to own the copyright until 21st April 1989, when the Really Useful Group purchased it for £1 million pounds.

A lavish new production of *Joseph*, with a revised score, opened at the London Palladium on June 2, 1991, with Jason Donovan in the title role. After an extensive tour of North America (featuring Donny Osmond), *Joseph* began a new Broadway run in 1993, with Michael Damian as the biblical hero, joining two other Lloyd Webber shows in New York, *Cats* and *The Phantom of the Opera*.

THE SUNDAY TIMES, 19 MAY 1968

Pop goes Joseph

JAZZ/POP
DEREK JEWELL

'GIVE US food' the brothers said,
'Dieting is for the birds.'
Joseph gave them all they wanted
Second helpings, even thirds...

EVEN ON paper the happy bounce of lyrics like these come through. They are exactly right for singing by several hundred boys' voices. With two organs, guitars, drums and a large orchestra the effect is irresistible.

The quicksilver vitality of **Joseph and His Amazing Technicolor Dreamcoat,** the new pop oratorio heard at Central Hall, Westminster, last Sunday, is attractive indeed. On this evidence the pop idiom—beat rhythms and Bacharachian melodies—is most enjoyably capable of being used in extended form.

Musically, "Joseph" is not all gold. It needs more light and shade. A very beautiful melody, "Close Every Door To Me" is one of the few points when the hectic pace slows down. The snap and crackle of the rest of the work tends to be too insistent, masking the impact of the words which, unlike many in pop, are important.

But such reservations seem pedantic when matched against "Joseph's" infectious overall character. Throughout its twenty-minute duration it bristles with wonderfully singable tunes. It entertains. It communicates instantly, as all good pop should. And it is a considerable piece of barrier-breaking by its creators, two men in their early twenties—Tim Rice, the lyricist, and Andrew Lloyd Webber, who wrote the music.

The performers last Sunday were the choir, school and orchestra of Colet Court, the St. Paul's junior school, with three solo singers and a pop group called The Mixed Bag. It was an adventurous experiment for a school, yet Alan Doggett, who conducted, produced a crisp, exciting and undraggy performance which emphasised the rich expansiveness of pop rather than the limitations of its frontiers.

TIM RICE
LYRICIST

Tim Rice was born in England in 1944. He won a Golden Globe and Oscar in 1993 for his composition with Alan Menken "A Whole New World", the love song from the Disney animated film **Aladdin**. In the theatre his work includes the book and lyrics of **Evita**, **Jesus Christ Superstar**, **Chess**, **Blondel**, and of course, **Joseph and the Amazing Technicolor Dreamcoat**. He recently adapted the French/Canadian musical **Starmania** for English-speaking audiences and the resulting album **Tycoon**, featuring among others Cyndi Lauper, Celine Dion and Tom Jones, has been a European hit. A stage show may follow. He is chairman of the Foundation for Sport and the Arts, an organization based in England that distributes over 60 million pounds annually to sporting and artistic causes in Great Britain. He recently completed the lyrics for the songs in the new Disney animated movie **The Lion King**, with music by Elton John, and is working on an album with Cliff Richard.

ANDREW LLOYD WEBBER
COMPOSER

Andrew Lloyd Webber was born in 1948. He is the composer of **Joseph and the Amazing Technicolor Dreamcoat** (1968, extended 1972), **Jesus Christ Superstar** (1971), the film scores of **Gumshoe** (1971) and the **Odessa File**, (1973), **Jeeves** (1974), **Evita** (1976), **Variations** (1978) and **Tell Me On A Sunday** (1979), combined as **Song & Dance** (1982), **Cats** (1981), **Starlight Express** (1984), **Requiem** (1985), a setting of the Latin Requiem Mass, **The Phantom of the Opera** (1986), **Aspects of Love** (1989) and **Sunset Boulevard** (1993).

His awards include four Tony Awards, four Drama Desk Awards, three Grammys, including the award for Best Classical Contemporary Composition for **Requiem** in 1986, and five Laurence Olivier awards.

He is the first person to have three musicals running in New York and three in London, a record he achieved in 1982 and again in January 1988. At that time he became the first recipient of the American Society of Composers, Authors and Publishers' Triple Play Award.

In September 1991 he surpassed all of his previous records and made theatre history by becoming the first person to have six shows running simultaneously in London's West End.

Andrew Lloyd Webber is also active as a producer, not only of his own, but of other writers' works. He has produced on Broadway **Shirley Valentine**, **Lend Me A Tenor**, **La Bête**. His revival of **Joseph and the Amazing Technicolor Dreamcoat** has opened in London, Canada, Australia, on Broadway and is currently touring the UK.

In 1988 he was awarded Fellowship of the Royal College of Music.

In 1992 he was awarded a Knighthood for services to the arts and in February 1993 he was given a Star on the Hollywood Walk of Fame.

His latest production, **Sunset Boulevard**, opened in Los Angeles in December of the same year, to huge acclaim. This new production is now playing in London where it too has received enormous critical approval.

JACOB AND SONS

Lyrics by TIM RICE
Music by ANDREW LLOYD WEBBER

Broadly (♩=112)

Faster (♩=144)
NARRATOR

accel.

Way, way back man-y cen-tur-ies a-go,
Ja-cob was the found-er of a whole new na-tion,

not long af-ter the Bi-ble be-gan,
thanks to the num-ber of chil-dren he'd had.

Ja-cob lived in the
He was al-so known as Is-ra-el but

land _ of Ca - naan, a fine ex - am - ple of a fam - i - ly man.
most. _ of the time _ his sons and his wives _ used to call _ him dad.

Ja - cob, Ja - cob and Sons, _ de - pend - ed on farm - ing to
Ja - cob, Ja - cob and Sons, _ men of the soil _ of the

earn _ their keep. Ja - cob, Ja - cob and Sons, _ spent
sheaf _ and crook. Ja - cob, Ja - cob and Sons, _ a re -

NARRATOR and BROTHERS

all of the days _ in the fields _ with sheep.
mark - a - ble fam - i - ly in an - y - one's book. Reu - ben was the eld - est of the

JOSEPH'S COAT

Lyrics by TIM RICE
Music by ANDREW LLOYD WEBBER

ONE MORE ANGEL IN HEAVEN

Lyrics by TIM RICE
Music by ANDREW LLOYD WEBBER

24

POTIPHAR

Lyrics by TIM RICE
Music by ANDREW LLOYD WEBBER

CHORUS

Po - ti - phar had ve - ry few cares. He was one of E - gypt's
Po - ti - phar was cool and so fine. But my wife would ne - ver

mil - lion - aires. Hav - ing made a for - tune buy - ing shares in Py - ra - mids.
toe the line. It's all there in chap - ter thir - ty - nine of Ge - ne - sis

CHORUS

Po - ti - phar had made a huge pile, owned a large per - cen - tage
She was beau - ti - ful but e - vil, saw a lot of men a -

29

2nd time

cross hands

Po - ti - phar was count-ing shek-els in his den be -

- low the bed-room, when he heard a migh-ty rum-pus clat-ter-ing a - bove him.

CLOSE EVERY DOOR

Lyrics by TIM RICE
Music by ANDREW LLOYD WEBBER

Da ℅ al Coda ⊕ e poi Coda

GO GO GO JOSEPH

Lyrics by TIM RICE
Music by ANDREW LLOYD WEBBER

38

SONG OF THE KING
(SEVEN FAT COWS)

Lyrics by TIM RICE
Music by ANDREW LLOYD WEBBER

THOSE CANAAN DAYS

Lyrics by TIM RICE
Music by ANDREW LLOYD WEBBER

Do you re - mem - ber the good years in Ca - naan?
mem - ber those won - der - ful par - ties?

The sum - mers were end - less - ly gold.
The splen - dour of Ca - naan's cui - sine.

The fields were a patch - work of clo - ver,
Our ex - trav - a - gant, el - e - gant soi - rées,

BENJAMIN CALYPSO

Lyrics by TIM RICE
Music by ANDREW LLOYD WEBBER

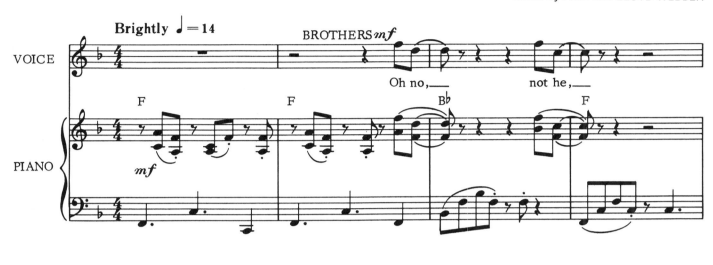

ANY DREAM WILL DO

Lyrics by TIM RICE
Music by ANDREW LLOYD WEBBER

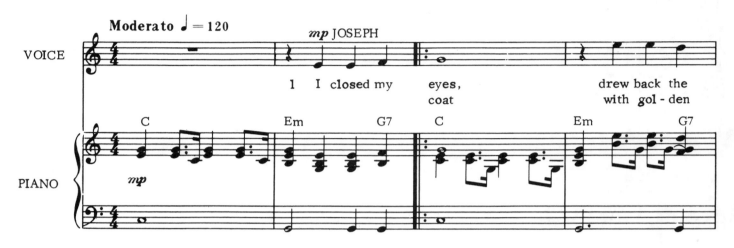